THE ILLUSTRATED
ENCYCLOPEDIA

VOLUME 3

E - F

Belitha Press

First published 1995 by
Macmillan Education Australia Pty Ltd

First published in the United Kingdom in 1995 by
Belitha Press Limited
31 Newington Green, London N16 9PU

Cataloguing in print data available from the British Library.

ISBN 1 85561 522 3 (Vol 3)
ISBN 1 85561 529 0 (Set)

Consultant: Frances Warhurst
UK editor: Maria O'Neill
Project editor: Jo Higgins

Typeset by Polar Design
Printed in Hong Kong

Acknowledgements

The author and publisher are grateful to the following for permission to reproduce copyright photographs:

Cover: Mantis Wildlife Films

Australian Red Cross, p. 35 (top right); Coo-ee Picture Library, pp. 5, 12, 14, 15, 17 (left), 19, 20, 22 (bottom left & right), 25 (bottom), 26 (bottom), 28 (bottom), 31 (top), 33, 39 (top & bottom left), 40 (bottom left), 42 (bottom left), 43, 49 (left), 51 (centre), 53 (bottom), 57 (left), 59 (top & centre), 62 (top); G & B Cheers/A.N.T. Photo Library, p. 64 (bottom); Brian Chudleigh/A.N.T. Photo Library, p. 60 (top); W. Fagan, p. 28 (top); Mantis Wildlife Films, p. 41 (bottom right); Northside Photographics, pp. 27 (left & top right), 35 (bottom), 51 (top); The Photo Library, pp. 8, 36 (top & bottom), 37 (right & bottom), 38 (bottom); Otto Rogge/A.N.T. Photo Library, p. 9; Silvestris/A.N.T. Photo Library, pp. 51 (bottom right), 55; Sporting Pix, p. 47 (bottom); South Australian Tourism Commission, p. 13; Ron & Valerie Taylor/A.N.T. Photo Library, p. 11; Tesselaar's Bulbs & Flowers, pp. 42 & 43.

While every care has been taken to trace and acknowledge copyright, the publishers tender their apologies for any accidental infringement where copyright has proved untraceable.

Illustrators

Sharyn Madder: 14, 18, 19, 30, 31, 48, 49, 50, 51, 54, 55, 58, 59
Rhyll Plant: 6, 7, 8, 9, 20, 36, 37, 52, 53, 60, 61, 64
John Fairbridge: 16, 17, 24, 25, 28, 29, 32, 33, 34, 35, 39, 44, 45, 56
Paul Konye: 12, 21, 38
Andrew Plant: 10, 11, 13, 15, 26, 40, 43, 46
Xiangyi Mo: 4, 5, 23, 63

HOW TO USE THIS BOOK

The Illustrated Encyclopedia has over 300 entries. The entries are arranged alphabetically. To find your topic, use the guide letters at the top of each page to check you have the right volume. The first letter of your topic will be highlighted.

TOPIC: EARS

guide letter

A B C D E F G H I J K L M

Use the guide words printed in the top right-hand corner of each page to find your topic. The guide words list the entries on a double-page spread. They are listed alphabetically. Check the guide words to see if you need to go backwards or forwards.

guide word

EARS

You can also use the index in Volume 9 to find your topic.

ears
    Volume 3 **4–5**
    Volume 7 57

If you cannot find your topic in its alphabetical order in the encyclopedia, use the index.

Europe
    see continent

TOPIC: EUROPE

The index lists all the topics in alphabetical order. It tells you where you will find your topic.

More information on how to use the encyclopedia and the index can be found in Volume 9.

EARS

SEE ALSO
• Bat • Brain • Dolphin
• Human Body • Sound

Our ears help us to hear and keep our balance. There are three parts to the ear – the outer ear, the inner ear and the middle ear.

PARTS OF THE EAR

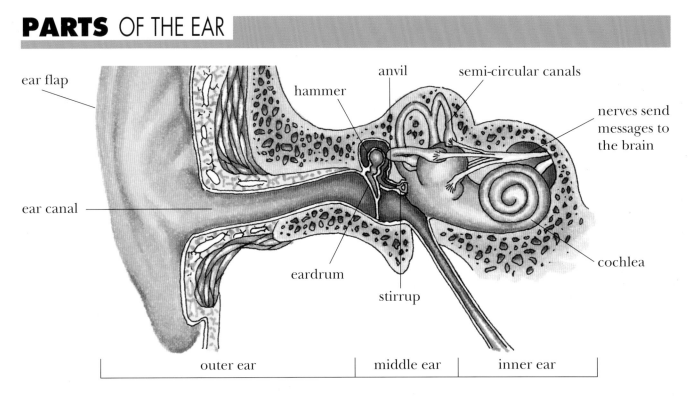

ear flap

ear canal

hammer

anvil

semi-circular canals

nerves send messages to the brain

eardrum

stirrup

cochlea

outer ear | middle ear | inner ear

• The outer ear is the part we can see and touch, and the ear canal going into our head. The outer ear is shaped to collect sounds.

• The middle ear makes these sounds stronger.

• The inner ear sends messages to the brain. The brain interprets what you are hearing. The inner ear also helps you to balance.

HOW YOUR EARS WORK

1. The outer ear catches soundwaves and sends them to the ear canal.
2. Soundwaves travel to the eardrums at the end of the ear canal. The eardrum is a piece of skin stretched across the middle ear. This skin vibrates with sound. The sound vibrations travel through three tiny bones to the cochlea. The three bones are the hammer, the anvil and the stirrup.
3. Nerve endings in the cochlea send messages to the brain. Your brain works out what you are hearing.

Sound is made by objects vibrating. It is carried on waves through the air.

KEEPING YOUR BALANCE

Your ears help you to keep your balance. The semi-circular canals of the inner ear are hollow and contain liquid. When you move, the liquid moves. Signals are sent to the brain to help you keep your balance.

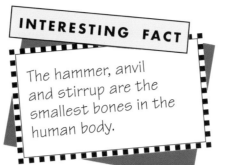

INTERESTING FACT

The hammer, anvil and stirrup are the smallest bones in the human body.

SIGN LANGUAGE

Deaf people cannot hear sounds. People can use sign language to talk to deaf people.

ANIMALS' EARS

Bats use their ears to navigate and find their food in the dark. This is called echolocation. Dolphins also use echolocation to find their way underwater.

An elephant's big ears help it to keep cool.

A rabbit can turn its ears to collect sounds without moving its head.

EARTH

SEE ALSO • Atmosphere • Desert • Mountain • Ocean • Planet

Earth is shaped like a giant ball. It is one of the nine planets which orbit the Sun. The Earth's surface is made of rock. It has four layers.

PARTS OF THE EARTH

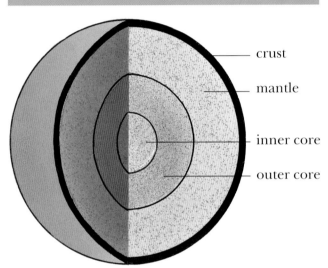

- crust
- mantle
- inner core
- outer core

- The crust is the solid outer layer. It is up to 70 kilometres deep below mountains, but only 6 kilometres thick under the sea.
- The mantle is made up of hot rocks. It is about 2900 kilometres thick.
- The outer core is made up of hot melted rock. It is about 2000 kilometres thick.
- The inner core is a solid ball of rock. It is much hotter than the outer core. It is about 2600 kilometres thick.

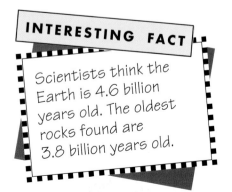

INTERESTING FACT

Scientists think the Earth is 4.6 billion years old. The oldest rocks found are 3.8 billion years old.

THE EARTH

The Earth looks blue from space. Nearly 70 per cent of the Earth's surface is covered by oceans or seas. Air surrounds the Earth.

Mountains cover 20 per cent of the Earth's surface.

Deserts cover 4 per cent of the Earth's surface.

THE EARTH'S MOVEMENT

The Earth is spinning as it travels around the Sun. It takes 24 hours (one day) to complete a spin. It takes 365¼ days to travel around the Sun.

Sun

Oceans cover 70 per cent of the Earth's surface.

Forests cover 25 per cent of the Earth's land surface.

The North and South Poles are the coldest places on Earth.

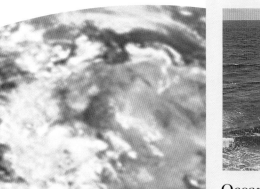

7

EARTHQUAKE

SEE ALSO • Earth • Tides • Volcano

An earthquake is when the Earth vibrates and trembles. Sometimes, wide cracks appear on the Earth's surface after an earthquake.

Earthquakes can cause great damage. Buildings and houses may fall apart and roads are wrecked.

HOW AN EARTHQUAKE HAPPENS

• The Earth's surface is made up of plates of rock.
• When one plate pushes against another, it causes deep cracks in the rock. The cracks are called fault lines.
• When the rocks move suddenly along the fault lines, an earthquake happens.

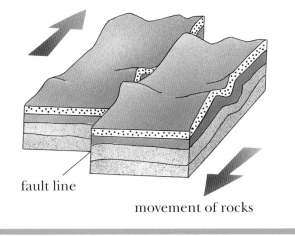

movement of rocks

fault line

movement of rocks

SEISMOLOGY

Seismology is the study of earthquakes. Scientists use machines to record movements in the Earth's surface. Many earthquakes only create minor tremors.

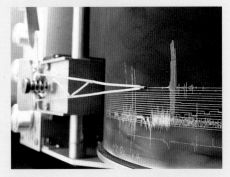

INTERESTING FACT

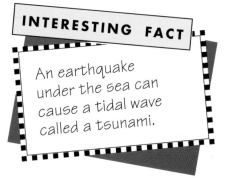

An earthquake under the sea can cause a tidal wave called a tsunami.

EARTHWORM

| SEE ALSO | • Animal • Compost • Invertebrate • Worm |

An earthworm is an animal.
It has a soft body and lives in damp soil.

PARTS OF AN EARTHWORM

A worm does not have ears or eyes.
It breathes through its skin.

saddle

mouth

body made up of segments

4 pairs of tiny bristles on each segment
except the first and last – bristles help
worms move through earth

Length: 1 millimetre to 3 metres

HOW EARTHWORMS LIVE

• Earthworms burrow into the soil, mixing
layers of earth. Their burrows create holes for
air and water.
• Earthworms eat soil. They help to break
down dead plant material. Their droppings are
called castings.
• Worms usually mate with another worm to
form eggs. After mating, eggs are laid in a
cocoon and left in the soil.
• Young worms hatch in two to five weeks.
They live for about a year.

FOOD

Dead plant material in
the soil.

HOW EARTHWORMS MOVE

An earthworm moves by stretching the
front part of its body in the direction it
wants to move. It then pulls up the back
part. The front part stretches out again.

ECHINODERM

SEE ALSO
• Animal • Invertebrate
• Seashore Life

An echinoderm is a sea animal. There are five kinds of echinoderms – starfish, brittle stars, sea urchins, sea cucumbers and sea-lilies.

Echinoderms do not have a head or tail. Their bodies have a circular shape. Their skin is often formed into spikes.

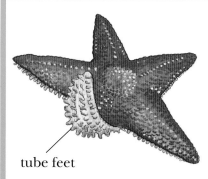

tube feet

HOW THEY MOVE

Echinoderms have hundreds of tube feet which often have suckers on the end. They use these tube feet to attach themselves to surfaces and to move.

STARFISH

Starfish usually have five arms. Some have 12 to 20 arms. They have rows of tube feet with suckers underneath. A starfish eats oysters, clams and other molluscs. It forces shells open with its tube feet and eats the food inside.

WHERE THEY LIVE

Echinoderms are found in the sea in all parts of the world except the seas of the North and South Poles.

INTERESTING FACT

A starfish can escape from an enemy by dropping an arm. A new arm will grow in a few weeks.

BRITTLE STARS

Brittle stars have five long, thin arms. A brittle star catches food with its arms.

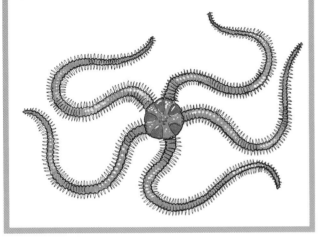

SEA-LILIES

Sea-lilies look like plants. Many sea-lilies are attached to the seabed by a long tube like a stalk. The mouth is surrounded by a flower of feathery tentacles which collect food. Some sea-lilies have no stalk. These sea-lilies float in the sea.

SEA URCHIN ▼

A sea urchin is made of chalky plates covered with spines. Sea urchins eat tiny animals and plants from rocks and the seabed. When a sea urchin dies, the skin and spines drop off, leaving a skeleton of plates on the bottom of the sea.

SEA CUCUMBERS ▼

Sea cucumbers have leathery skin. Some sea cucumbers catch small animals. Others scoop up mud and eat bits of food in it.

ECLIPSE

SEE ALSO
• Earth • Moon • Planet
• Sun

An eclipse is when a moon or planet moves into the shadow of another moon or planet. Eclipses happen because all the planets in the solar system are moving.

AN ECLIPSE OF THE SUN

A solar eclipse happens when the Moon passes between the Earth and the Sun, blocking out the Sun's light. The Moon's shadow falls on the Earth and the sky looks black during the day. When the Moon's shadow passes, daylight returns.

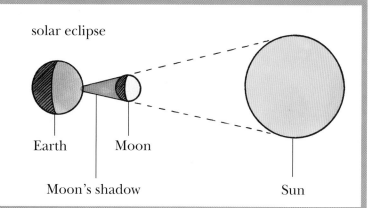

solar eclipse

Earth   Moon

Moon's shadow   Sun

AN ECLIPSE OF THE MOON

A lunar eclipse happens when the Earth is between the Moon and the Sun. The Earth's shadow falls on the Moon.

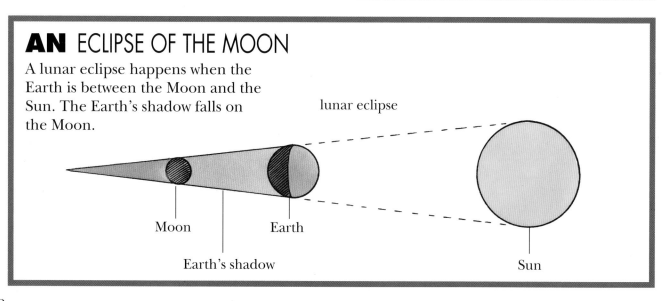

lunar eclipse

Moon   Earth

Earth's shadow   Sun

ECOLOGY

SEE ALSO
• Conservation • Food Chain
• Pollution

Ecology is the study of living things and how they live together in their environment. Ecology is also the study of non-living things, such as soil, air and water, and how they affect living things.

AN ECOSYSTEM

An ecosystem is a group of animals and plants, and their non-living environment. There are many different kinds of ecosystems – ponds, forests, aquariums, oceans, rivers and coral reefs.

A FOOD CHAIN

The Sun provides energy for all living things. Plants are the beginning of a food chain.

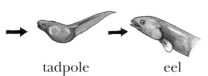

Sun   pond weed   tadpole   eel

CHANGES IN AN ECOSYSTEM

If some kinds of living things die out, other living things can lose their food supply and may die out also.

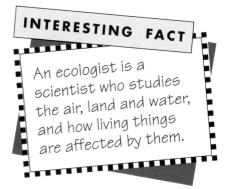

INTERESTING FACT

An ecologist is a scientist who studies the air, land and water, and how living things are affected by them.

A FOOD WEB

Plants and animals are linked in a food web. A food web is several food chains linked together in an ecosystem.

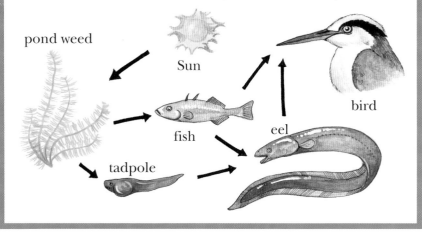

pond weed

Sun

fish

bird

eel

tadpole

13

EEL

SEE ALSO • Animal • Fish • Fishing

An eel is a fish. It has a long, thin body.
Eels can live in fresh water and salt water.
There are many different kinds of eels.

PARTS OF AN EEL

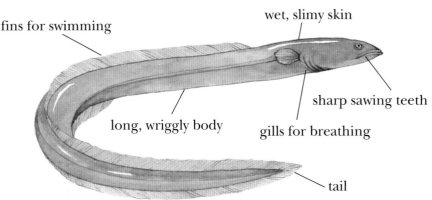

fins for swimming

wet, slimy skin

long, wriggly body

sharp sawing teeth

gills for breathing

tail

Length: 15 centimetres to 4 metres

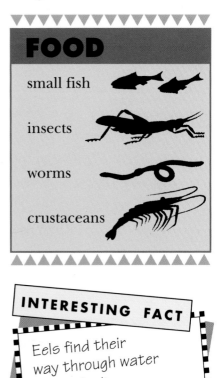

FOOD

small fish

insects

worms

crustaceans

Young eels are born in the Sargasso Sea and swim back to fresh water in Europe and North America.

HOW EELS LIVE

• Eels that live in fresh water breed in the sea.
• European and American freshwater eels swim thousands of kilometres to the Sargasso Sea to breed.
• The parent eels die after laying their eggs.
• The young eels are called elvers. It takes the elvers three years to swim back to the rivers.

INTERESTING FACT

Eels find their way through water by instinct.

EGG

SEE ALSO • Animal • Life Cycle

An egg is the beginning of most animal life. Eggs are produced by the female animal. The egg must be fertilized before it can grow. It must be joined with a sperm cell from the male animal. This happens when animals mate.

DIFFERENT KINDS OF EGGS

Most animals lay eggs. The egg contains food for the young animal. Female birds, insects, fish, reptiles and amphibians lay eggs outside their bodies.

frog eggs

butterfly eggs

earthworm eggs

turtle egg

fish eggs

bird egg

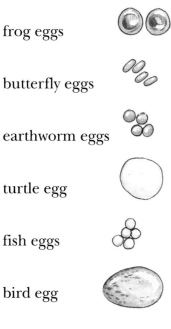

◄ BIRDS

Birds lay hard-shelled eggs. The baby bird develops inside the egg before it hatches.

REPTILES

Snakes and lizards lay eggs which have leathery shells. Crocodiles and tortoises lay eggs which have hard shells.

MAMMALS ►

In most mammals, the egg is very small. It stays inside the mother's body. The young mammal gets food from its mother's body. When it is born, it feeds on its mother's milk.

MONOTREMES

Monotremes are mammals that lay eggs. The echidna and the platypus lay eggs. After about ten days, the young hatch out of the eggs and feed on their mother's milk.

ELECTRICITY

| SEE ALSO | • Coal • Fuel • Gas • Oil • Water |

Electricity is a form of energy. It provides energy for lighting and heating. It also powers many different machines in the home.

Electricity can provide power to light up cities, drive trains, operate huge machines in factories or light a bulb.

HOW ELECTRICITY WORKS

• Electricity flows through wires as an electric current. The electric current can only flow if a wire makes a complete loop called a circuit.
• The electric current stops moving when there is a gap in the circuit.
• A switch opens and closes gaps in circuits.

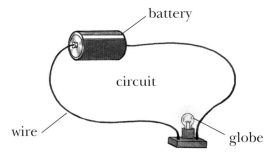

battery

circuit

wire

globe

Electricity is the movement of tiny particles cailed electrons. Electrons carry tiny electric charges. When a wire is connected to a source of electricity, the electric charges flow along the wire.

USES OF ELECTRICITY IN THE HOME

washing machine

refrigerator

computer

telephone

heater

light

kettle

toaster

television

HOW ELECTRICITY GETS TO THE HOME

The electricity we use in our houses is produced by huge electric generators in power stations. The generators are often driven by steam produced by burning coal, oil or gas, or by nuclear power.

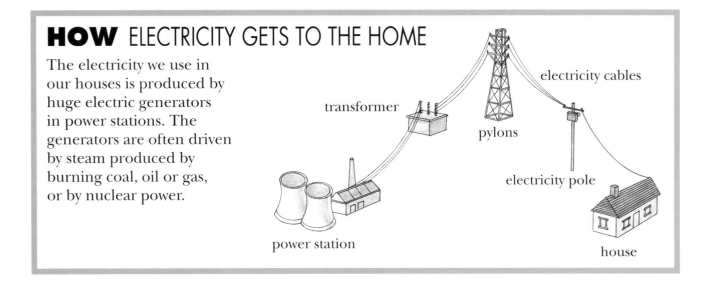

transformer

electricity cables

pylons

electricity pole

power station

house

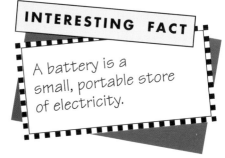

INTERESTING FACT

A battery is a small, portable store of electricity.

HYDRO-ELECTRIC ▶ POWER STATIONS

Hydro-electric power stations use the energy of fast flowing water to produce electricity.

ELECTRICIANS

Electricians know how electricity works. They can install electricity in our homes and repair machines that are powered by electricity.

ELEPHANT

SEE ALSO • Animal • Endangered Species • Mammal

An elephant is the largest land animal. Elephants are very strong. They have a good memory and never forget anything they learn.

PARTS OF AN ELEPHANT

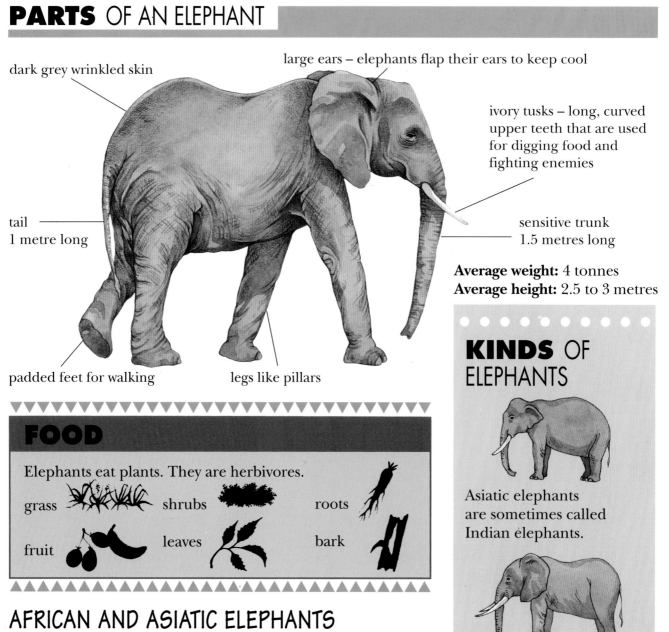

dark grey wrinkled skin

large ears – elephants flap their ears to keep cool

ivory tusks – long, curved upper teeth that are used for digging food and fighting enemies

tail
1 metre long

padded feet for walking

legs like pillars

sensitive trunk
1.5 metres long

Average weight: 4 tonnes
Average height: 2.5 to 3 metres

KINDS OF ELEPHANTS

Asiatic elephants are sometimes called Indian elephants.

African elephants

FOOD

Elephants eat plants. They are herbivores.

grass   shrubs   roots

fruit   leaves   bark

AFRICAN AND ASIATIC ELEPHANTS

- The African elephant has bigger tusks and larger ears than the Asiatic elephant. It has a different-shaped back.
- African elephants are usually bigger than Asiatic elephants.

HOW ELEPHANTS LIVE

• Elephants live in herds of up to 1000. They communicate with each other using touch and different sounds.

• One calf is born at a time. It can walk several hours after birth. It drinks milk from its mother's teat. The calf starts to eat grass and other plants when it is two to six years old. The mother elephant stays close to her calf and protects it until it becomes an adult.

• Elephants live for about 60 years.

WHERE ELEPHANTS LIVE

● Asia
■ Africa

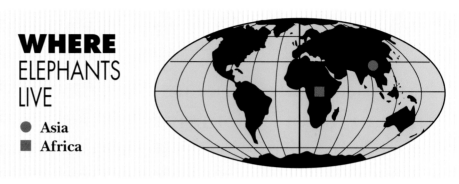

INTERESTING FACT

Elephants usually eat for about 16 hours a day. They travel hundreds of kilometres to find food or water.

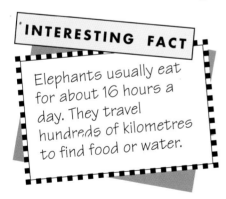

AN ELEPHANT'S TRUNK

An elephant's trunk is a combined nose and upper lip. An elephant uses its trunk to:

• eat and drink
• breathe and smell
• stroke its mate and young
• carry loads
• hold an enemy during fighting
• give itself a shower to keep cool.

AN ENDANGERED SPECIES

Over the years, elephants have been hunted for their tusks. Today, elephants are an endangered species and there are laws to protect them.

19

ENDANGERED SPECIES

SEE ALSO
• Conservation • Ecology
• National Park • Panda • Zoo

An endangered species is an animal or plant which is in danger of becoming extinct. Extinct means that a species of animal or plant will die out and never live on the Earth again.

WHY ANIMALS AND PLANTS BECOME ENDANGERED

- People destroy the places where plants and animals live.
- People hunt animals.
- Pollution poisons the food chain.

RESERVES

National parks and reserves are areas set up for breeding endangered animals such as tigers.

◀ THE PANDA

The panda bear is an endangered animal. Its habitat is being destroyed.

THE DODO

The dodo is a bird that became extinct in the 1800s. Dodos lived on the island of Mauritius in the Indian Ocean. Sailors hunted and killed dodos for food.

HOW WE CAN HELP

- Do not buy products made from wild animals.
- Be sure your pets have been bred and raised in captivity.
- Support zoos that are breeding endangered animals, by visiting them.
- Learn as much as possible about nature and teach others what you know.
- Reduce pollution to stop damaging the environment.
- Recycle resources.

EQUATOR

SEE ALSO • Continent • Earth • Latitude and Longitude

The equator is an imaginary line around the middle of the Earth. The middle of the Earth is the widest part.

THE HEMISPHERES

The equator divides the Earth into two equal parts – the Northern Hemisphere and the Southern Hemisphere.

• Europe, Asia, North America and northern Africa are in the Northern Hemisphere.

• Australia, Antarctica, South America and southern Africa are in the Southern Hemisphere.

North Pole

Northern Hemisphere

equator

Southern Hemisphere

South Pole

CIRCUMFERENCE

The equator is 40 091 kilometres measured from one spot, right around and back to the same spot. This is the circumference of the Earth.

DAY AND NIGHT

The Earth is hottest at the equator because the Sun's rays shine directly on places near the equator.

DIAMETER

The equator measures 12 757 kilometres through the centre of the Earth. This is the diameter of the Earth.

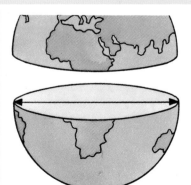

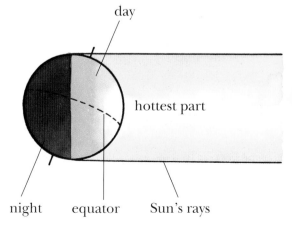

day

hottest part

night   equator   Sun's rays

EXERCISE

SEE ALSO • Gymnastics • Human Body

Exercise helps to keep your heart and lungs healthy and your muscles strong. Walking, running, swimming, cycling and gymnastics are different kinds of exercise.

OUT OF BREATH?

When you exercise, you breathe more quickly. When you cannot breathe in enough oxygen to keep you going, you become tired. If you exercise regularly, you can increase the amount of oxygen that your body receives. This helps you to exercise for longer periods of time.

WARMING UP

Always start exercising by doing some gentle stretching exercises to warm the muscles. This prevents injuries.

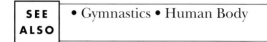

INTERESTING FACT

There are over 600 muscles in your body.

TRAINING

You can spend many hours training and strengthening your muscles. Gymnasts exercise lots of different muscles in their bodies.

EYE

SEE ALSO
• Camera • Human Body
• Light

Our eyes see everything around us. They let us know the colour, shape and size of the things we can see.

PARTS OF OUR EYE

Eyelids and eyelashes keep dust and dirt out of your eyes.

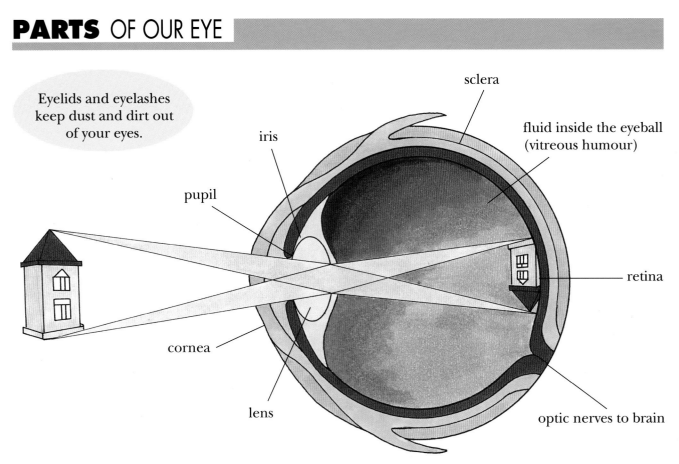

sclera

fluid inside the eyeball (vitreous humour)

iris

pupil

retina

cornea

lens

optic nerves to brain

HOW YOUR EYES WORK

• The pupil lets in light. Behind the pupil is a lens. The lens puts a picture of what you are looking at on to the back of the retina. The picture on the retina is upside down and back-to-front.

• Optic nerves take messages from the retina to the brain. The brain receives the messages. The brain can unscramble the picture you see so you can see it the right way up.

Light enters your eyes through the pupil. In bright light, the pupil gets smaller. In dim light, the pupil gets larger to let in as much light as possible.

INTERESTING FACT

Every time we blink, our eyes are washed with tears. Tears come from tiny sacs behind the eyes.

FARMING

| SEE ALSO | • Cattle • Cotton • Fishing • Nut • Vegetable |

Farming is an important industry. A farm is a place where animals are raised and crops are grown. Farmers provide us with food from their animals and crops.

FARM MACHINES

Long ago, machines were invented to do the work of people and animals.

tractor – pulls all kinds of farm machinery

Farmers in some countries cannot afford machines. They use simple tools. ▼

ORGANIC FARMS

Organic farmers do not use artificial pesticides and fertilizers.

plough – breaks the soil into furrows for planting

seed drill – puts seed in the soil and covers it

combine harvester – cuts crops and prepares them for storage

CEREAL CROPS

Rice, wheat and maize are cereal crops.
Cereal crops are the most important food crops.

LIVESTOCK

Cattle, pigs, sheep, goats, chickens and fish are livestock. They are raised by farmers to provide food for people.

FRUIT AND VEGETABLES

Fruit and vegetable crops are grown on farms. Farmers take their produce to market for us to buy and eat.

OTHER CROPS

Many other crops are grown on farms all over the world.

- Coffee, sugar, tea and cocoa are grown in warm countries.
- Seeds such as sunflower seeds, nuts and palms are grown for their oil. The oil is used in cooking and to make paint.
- Some crops such as clover and grass provide food for livestock.
- Some crops such as cotton and flax are grown to produce fibre. The fibre is used to make cloth, carpet, paper and rope.

FERN

A fern is a plant. Ferns were one of the first plants to grow on the Earth. Ferns do not have flowers or seeds. They grow in damp, shady places all over the world.

SEE ALSO • Coal • Forest • Plant • Rain Forest

FRONDS

Fern leaves are called fronds. They slowly uncurl as they grow.

KINDS OF FERNS

There are more than 10 000 different kinds of ferns. Some are small moss-like plants; others are tall like trees.

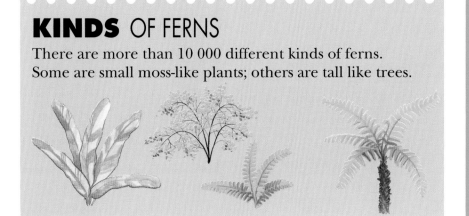

HOW FERNS GROW

- Tiny cells called spores are under the leaves.
- When they ripen, the wind scatters the spores.
- Each spore grows into a tiny plant called a prothallus.
- Male and female cells grow on the prothallus.
- When the cells are fertilized, the prothallus grows into a new fern.

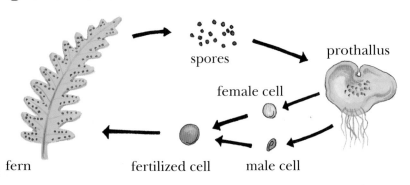

spores

prothallus

female cell

fern

fertilized cell

male cell

INTERESTING FACT

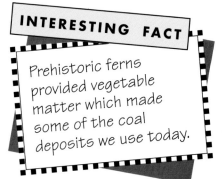

Prehistoric ferns provided vegetable matter which made some of the coal deposits we use today.

FESTIVAL

SEE ALSO • Dancing • Dragon

A festival is a time for celebration. Festivals can be a time for feasts, singing and dancing. They can be a quiet time for remembering. A festival can honour great leaders, gods or saints.

CHRISTMAS

Christmas is a Christian festival. Christians celebrate the birth of Jesus. In a nativity play, they act out the events leading up to the birth of Jesus.

◀ RAMADAN

Solemn festivals are times when people meditate and pray. Ramadan is the month of fasting for Muslims. They celebrate the end of Ramadan with a feast.

HANUKKAH

Hanukkah is a Jewish festival. The candles are lit one by one over the eight-day celebration.

DIWALI ▲

Diwali is a Hindu festival of light. Families place lights in windows to invite the goddess of light into their homes.

CARNIVALS

In some countries, many people celebrate festivals with carnivals and processions in the streets. People dress up, sing, dance and have fun.

27

FIREFIGHTERS

SEE ALSO
• Earthquake • Flood
• Police

A firefighter is a person who is trained to put out fires. Firefighters also rescue people who are trapped in burning buildings.

FIRE-ENGINES

A fire-engine carries pumps, hose lines, ladders and large tanks of water to a fire. Some trucks carry foam and water sprays for petrol fires.

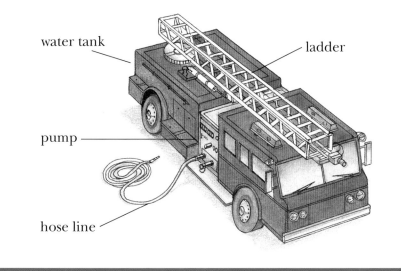

water tank

ladder

pump

hose line

FIRE STATIONS

Most towns have a fire station. Fire-engines and equipment are always ready for an emergency.

FIRE ALARMS ▶

A fire alarm alerts the firefighters. Within minutes, they rush to a fire.

FLOOD RESCUE

Firefighters help people during other disasters such as floods and earthquakes.

VOLUNTEER FIREFIGHTERS

Many people train to fight fires. They help firefighters during emergencies.

FIRE FIGHTING EQUIPMENT

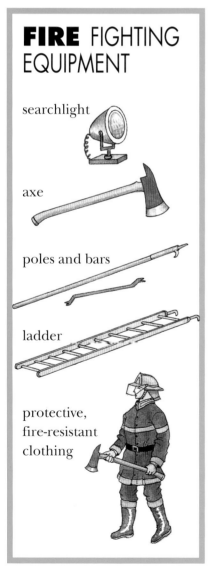

searchlight

axe

poles and bars

ladder

protective, fire-resistant clothing

RESCUING PEOPLE

Firefighters can rescue people trapped in buildings, with ladders or life nets.

FISH

| SEE ALSO | • Animal • Camouflage • Vertebrate |

A fish is an animal that lives in water. Some fish live in salt water, while others live in fresh water. Some fish live in both salt water and fresh water.

PARTS OF A FISH

scales

fin

tail fin

mouth

gill cover protects the gills

lateral line for detecting vibrations in water

WHERE FISH LIVE

Fish live in water all over the world.

HOW FISH BREATHE

Fish use gills to breathe oxygen from the water. Water is drawn in through the mouth and passed over the gill membranes. Oxygen is taken into the blood and carbon dioxide is removed.

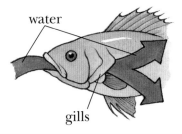

water

gills

FOOD

Some fish eat other water animals. They are carnivores. Some fish are plant-eaters (herbivores).

shellfish

worms

algae

HOW FISH SWIM

Fish swim forwards by bending their bodies from side to side and swinging their tail fins. They use their fins to steer and balance.

FINS

Fish use their fins to:
- stop their bodies rolling in the water
- stop
- turn
- push their bodies along.

HOW FISH LIVE

• Female fish lay eggs. Male fish fertilize the eggs. Fish hatch from the eggs.
• Most fish leave their eggs and newly hatched fish unprotected.
• Some fish such as sharks look after their young.

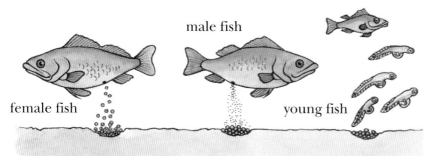

male fish

female fish

young fish

eggs

KINDS OF FISH

There are about 30 000 kinds of fish. Fish come in all sizes, shapes and colours. There are three groups of fish.
• Bony fish have a bony skeleton.
• Cartilaginous fish have a skeleton made of gristle.
• Jawless fish have no jaw.

SWIM BLADDER

• Most bony fish have a swim (air) bladder in their bodies. This keeps the fish at a certain level in the water.
• Cartilaginous fish do not have a swim bladder. If they stop swimming, they sink.

PROTECTION ▶

Some fish blend into their surroundings. Other fish can swim very fast to get away from their enemies.

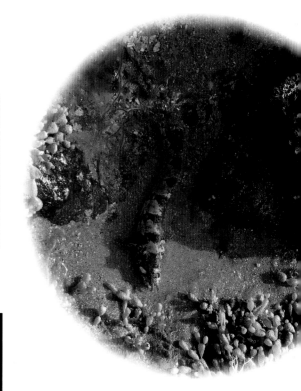

◀ DANGEROUS FISH

Some fish are dangerous. Stonefish, butterfly cod and catfish have poisonous spikes. Some fish are poisonous if people eat them. Some sharks are dangerous because they attack people.

FISHING

SEE ALSO
• Boat • Crab • Fish • Oyster
• Shark

Fishing is an important industry. It provides food for people all over the world. Fish are also used to make fish oil and fertilizers.

KINDS OF FISH USED FOR FOOD

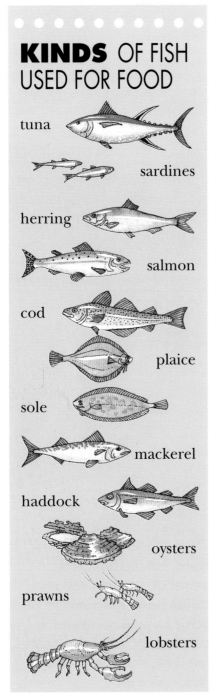

tuna

sardines

herring

salmon

cod

plaice

sole

mackerel

haddock

oysters

prawns

lobsters

SEA FISHING

Most fish are caught in nets.

- Trawl nets are long, bag-shaped nets which are dragged under the water.

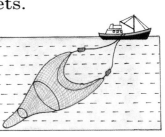

- Purse seine nets are large nets which are drawn around a shoal of fish to trap them.

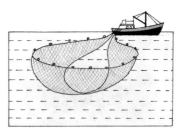

- Gill nets are like curtains that drift in the water. Fish swim into them and are caught in the mesh.

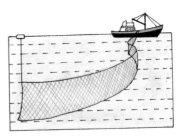

- Lining or trolling is when fish are caught on baited hooks. Lobsters are caught in traps.

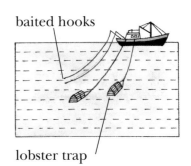

baited hooks

lobster trap

FISHING ▼ FLEETS

Most fish are caught at sea. Some fishing fleets fish in waters far from the shore. The fishing fleets stay out at sea for weeks at a time. They can store their catches in freezers.

FISHING FOR A HOBBY

Some people like to fish for fun and sport. You can fish from land or a boat. All you need is a line, a hook and some bait.

FISH CONSERVATION

• The fish in our seas and rivers are a valuable resource.

• Fishing needs to be controlled. If not, the number of fish will fall as there are fewer fish to breed.

• Countries have programmes and laws to prevent some kinds of fish becoming scarce from over-fishing.

FISH FARMS

Some fish such as trout, salmon and carp are bred in fish farms. Farmers sell the fish when they have grown big enough.

FLAG

SEE ALSO
• Knight • Olympic Games
• Pirate • Ship

A flag is a symbol for a group, a person or a country. It is made from a rectangular piece of cloth. Flags have bright colours and designs. They can be flown from poles and masts.

HISTORY

Long ago, streamers and banners were used as flags. They had different shapes and colours.

FLAGS AT SEA

Ships fly the flag of the country they come from. Sailors use semaphore flags to send messages from one ship to another.

FLAGS AROUND THE WORLD

Every country has its own flag. The colours and symbols on flags have special meanings.

FLAGS FOR GROUPS

Groups such as the United Nations and the Red Cross have their own flag.

The Red Cross often works in areas of danger. Their flag identifies the Red Cross and lets people know they are there to help. ▼

FLEA

SEE ALSO • Animal • Insect

A flea is a tiny insect. Fleas live on birds and animals. Some fleas can live on people. There are many different kinds of fleas.

PARTS OF A FLEA

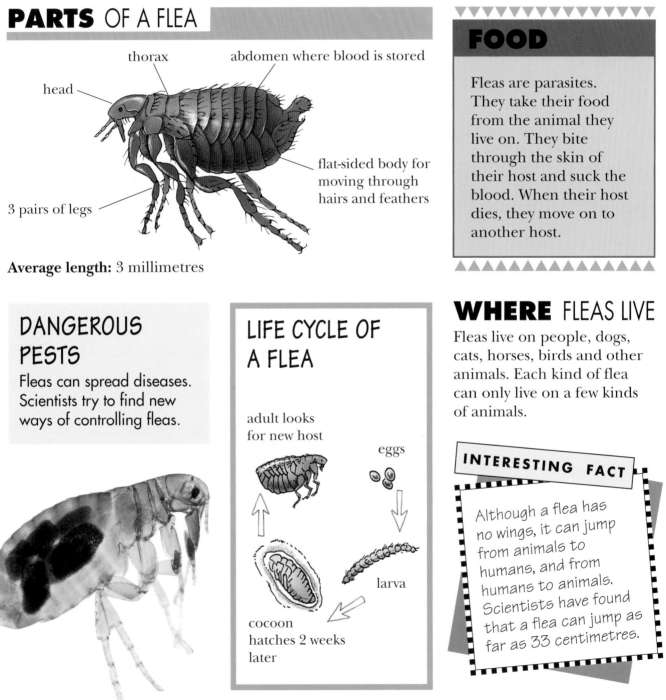

thorax

abdomen where blood is stored

head

3 pairs of legs

flat-sided body for moving through hairs and feathers

Average length: 3 millimetres

FOOD

Fleas are parasites. They take their food from the animal they live on. They bite through the skin of their host and suck the blood. When their host dies, they move on to another host.

DANGEROUS PESTS

Fleas can spread diseases. Scientists try to find new ways of controlling fleas.

LIFE CYCLE OF A FLEA

adult looks for new host

eggs

larva

cocoon hatches 2 weeks later

WHERE FLEAS LIVE

Fleas live on people, dogs, cats, horses, birds and other animals. Each kind of flea can only live on a few kinds of animals.

INTERESTING FACT

Although a flea has no wings, it can jump from animals to humans, and from humans to animals. Scientists have found that a flea can jump as far as 33 centimetres.

FLIES

SEE ALSO • Animal • Insect

Flies are insects with wings. There are many kinds of flies. The best known is the common house fly. Flies live all over the world. They are fast flying insects.

PARTS OF A FLY

head   thorax   1 pair of wings

antennae

eyes

abdomen

sponge-like
mouth parts

A fly breathes through air holes called spiracles along both sides of its body.

DANGEROUS PESTS

Many flies are dangerous to people. They carry germs. When a fly touches or bites us, it leaves behind germs it has picked up from rotting food. Scientists have developed ways to control flies.

LIFE CYCLE OF A FLY

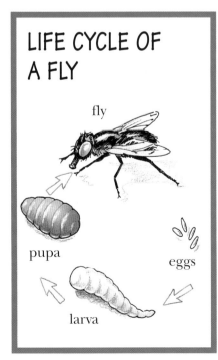

fly

pupa

larva

eggs

COMPOUND EYES

A fly has two large compound eyes made up of thousands of six-sided lenses.

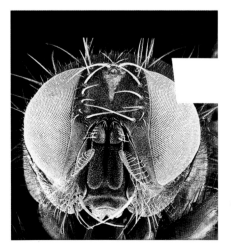

INTERESTING FACT

A fly can be airborne as soon as it beats its wings.

FLOATING

| SEE ALSO | • Boat • Pollution • Ship • Submarine |

When an object rests on the surface of water, it is floating. Floating depends on how much water an object pushes out of the way.

Objects that push lots of water out of the way receive an upward push from the water. This push supports the object so that it floats.

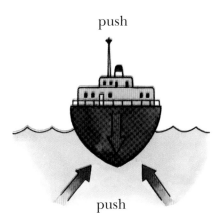

push

push

SHIP AT SEA ▲

A large ship pushes a lot of water out of the way. It gets a very strong push from the sea.

SOME LIQUIDS ▼ FLOAT

Liquids can float or sink depending on their density. Oil that spills from tankers floats on the sea because it is lighter than sea water. Most of the oil is washed up on to the shore and must be cleaned up.

FLOATING AND SINKING

If objects are heavy for their size, they will sink. If they are light for their size, they will float.

A solid ball of clay will sink.

If the same ball of clay is made into a boat shape with high sides, it will float.

AIR HELPS OBJECTS TO FLOAT

Water wings are full of air. They help children float in water.

FLOOD

SEE ALSO • Dam • Lake • River

A flood is a great amount of water flowing over dry land. Land can be flooded by water from rivers, lakes or the sea. Floods can cause great damage.

RIVER ▶ FLOODS

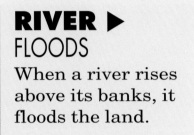

When a river rises above its banks, it floods the land.

LAKE FLOODS

Storms and winds can cause floods along the shores of lakes.

SEA COAST FLOODS

At sea, fierce storms can create great waves which flood the land along the coast.

FLOOD CONTROL ▶

Engineers are finding new ways to prevent floods. Barriers such as dams, dykes (high walls) and levees help keep water off the land.

FLOWER

SEE ALSO
• Bee • Bird • Fruit • Garden
• Nut • Plant • Rain Forest

A flower is the part of a plant where the seed grows. A new plant grows from a seed. Flowers come in different sizes, shapes and colours.

PARTS OF A FLOWER

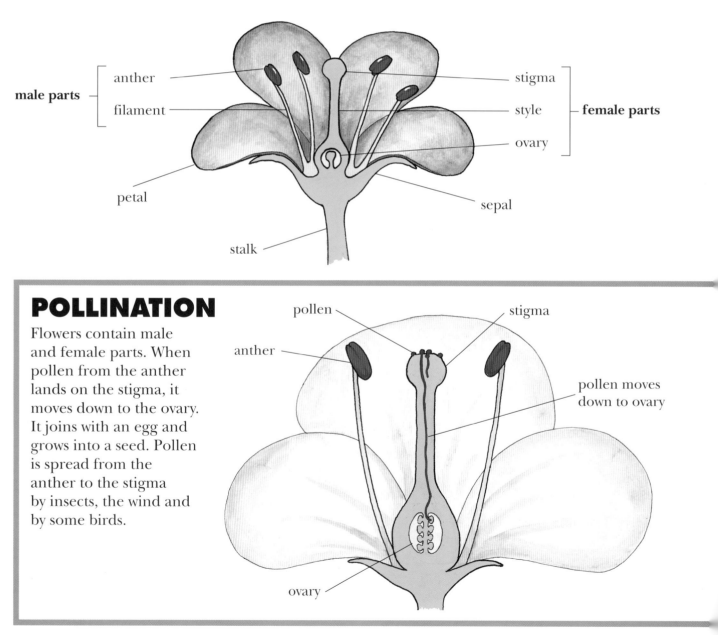

male parts
anther
filament

stigma
style
female parts
ovary

petal

sepal

stalk

POLLINATION

Flowers contain male and female parts. When pollen from the anther lands on the stigma, it moves down to the ovary. It joins with an egg and grows into a seed. Pollen is spread from the anther to the stigma by insects, the wind and by some birds.

pollen

stigma

anther

pollen moves down to ovary

ovary

FLOWER

A FLOWERING PLANT

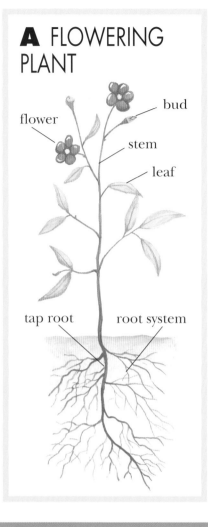

- flower
- bud
- stem
- leaf
- tap root
- root system

WHERE FLOWERS GROW

Flowers grow everywhere except in Antarctica.

- Flowers grow in forests where it is damp and shady.
- Flowers grow in deserts where it is very hot.
- Flowers grow in rain forests.
- Flowers grow in cold places.

SCENT ▶

A flower's scent attracts butterflies, bees and other pollinators.

FLOWERS ARE IMPORTANT

- Flowers produce grains, fruit and vegetables. These provide food for people and animals.
- Flowers decorate our gardens and houses.
- Flowers provide scent which is used to make perfume.

◀ Flowers pollinated by the wind usually have:

- dull colours
- anthers with pollen on long filaments which can fly in the air.

Flowers pollinated by ▶ insects and birds usually have:

- bright colours
- scent
- nectar.

Bees and other insects pollinate flowers as they travel from plant to plant in search of pollen and nectar.

WILD FLOWERS

Wild flowers are the flowers that have always grown in a particular place. In many countries, special areas and parks are set up to protect some wild flowers.

BULBS ▼

Some flowers such as tulips grow from bulbs.

FLOWERS AS SYMBOLS

Flowers are often used as a symbol for an area or country. The rose is the symbol for England.

42

WATER FLOWERS

A few flowers live on water. Waterlilies have large, flat leaves that can float on water.

pansy

◀ ANNUALS

Some flowers are called annuals. They only live for one growing season. You need to plant them every year to grow new flowers.

ORCHIDS ▶

Orchids grow well in tropical areas where it is hot and the air is moist.

INTERESTING FACT

Grass is a flowering plant. Grass flowers do not have colourful petals or a scent.

FLOWER FARM

Some flowers are grown on farms. The scent from the flowers is used to make perfume. Other flowers are grown on farms and sent to markets for people to buy.

FOOD

| SEE ALSO | • Digestion • Fruit • Plant • Vegetable • Vitamins |

Food is all the things we eat. All living things need food to grow. Food comes from plants and animals.

KINDS OF FOOD

There are three main kinds of food: proteins, fats and carbohydrates.

Proteins

Proteins build and repair cells. They keep bones, muscles and skin healthy.

eggs

lentils

beans

cheese

nuts

lean meat

peas

fish

milk

Fats and carbohydrates

Fats and carbohydrates are fuel foods. These foods give our body energy.

Fats

cream

butter

oil

Carbohydrates

bread

potatoes

rice

cake

Our bodies also need vitamins and minerals in small amounts. We can get these from eating a healthy diet.

A HEALTHY, BALANCED DIET

Your body needs lots of different foods while you are growing. If you eat more than your daily energy needs, your body will put on weight.

In some countries, many people do not have enough food to eat.

Tuna reduced salt

Baked Bea

Red Lentils   Borlotti Beans   Split Peas   Dried Pea   Brow

A VEGETARIAN DIET

A vegetarian diet is based on vegetables. It does not include meat and fish. Some vegetarians do not eat cheese, butter and eggs. A vegan is a person who only eats food from plants. A balanced vegetarian diet can be very healthy.

METHODS OF PRESERVING FOOD

canning

drying

bottling

freezing

conserving

NATIONAL FOOD

Many of the foods we like to eat are from different countries.

curry from India

sushi from Japan

chow mein from China

spaghetti from Italy

shish kebab from Turkey

chilli con carne from Mexico

SHARING ▶ FOOD

It is fun to share a meal with family and friends.

FOOD CHAIN

SEE ALSO
• Conservation • Ecology
• Plant • Pollution

A food chain shows how energy is passed on from one living thing to another. All living things need food for energy.

Sun

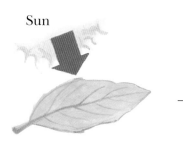

The Sun gives energy to the leaf.

The leaf gives energy to the caterpillar.

The caterpillar gives energy to the bird.

Sun

The Sun provides algae with energy.

Algae are food for tadpoles.

Tadpoles are food for trout.

Trout are food for cormorants.

A LEAF MAKES ITS OWN FOOD

A leaf is like a small factory.
It uses water, carbon dioxide and sunlight.
The sunlight is the energy which is used to change water and carbon dioxide into food.
Plants are food for all living things.

FOOTBALL

SEE ALSO   • Rugby • Soccer

Football is a sport. Two teams of players try to control a ball. Each team tries to get the ball down to the other end of the field to score goals or points.

KINDS OF FOOTBALL

Many different kinds of football are played around the world. The main differences are the size of the ball, the number of players and the rules.
- Soccer
- American Rules
- Rugby Union
- Rugby League
- Australian Rules
- Gaelic Football
- Canadian Football

People who play football are usually very fit. They play as part of a team and have good ball skills.

SPECTATOR SPORT ▶
All over the world, football is a popular game. Huge crowds watch their favourite teams play.

FOREST

SEE ALSO
- Animal • Ecology
- National Park • Rain Forest

A forest is a large area of land covered with trees. Many types of plants grow in a forest. Forests provide a home for many different animals. Some live on the forest floor; others live in plants and trees.

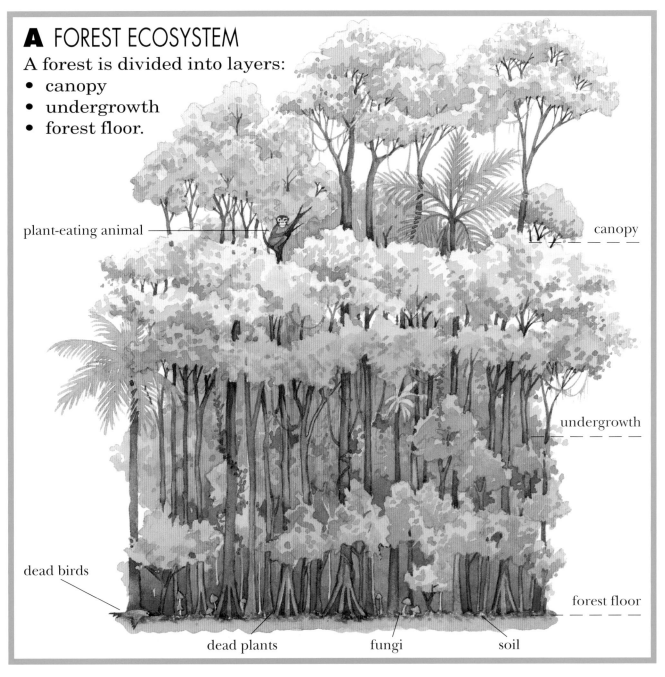

A FOREST ECOSYSTEM

A forest is divided into layers:
- canopy
- undergrowth
- forest floor.

plant-eating animal

canopy

undergrowth

dead birds

forest floor

dead plants   fungi   soil

Many different plants and animals live in a forest. They interact with each other and with the forest environment in which they live.

1. Plants need air, moisture, Sun, soil and minerals to grow.

2. Green plants produce food.

3. Some animals eat plants. Other animals eat the animals that eat plants.

4. Bacteria and fungi break down the remains of dead plants and animals. The broken-down material is used by plants for growth.

KINDS OF FORESTS

There are three main kinds of forest.

Softwood forests
Softwood forests grow mostly in cold, northern regions. These forests mainly have coniferous trees. Coniferous trees grow cones. They are evergreen. Pine trees grow in softwood forests.

Tropical forests
Tropical forests grow mostly near the equator in hot steamy regions. Ebony and mahogany trees grow in tropical forests.

Hardwood forests
Hardwood forests grow mostly in warm, moist regions. These forests mainly have deciduous trees. Deciduous trees lose their leaves in autumn and grow new leaves in spring. Walnut trees grow in hardwood forests.

WHERE
FORESTS GROW

- softwood forests
- hardwood forests
- tropical forests

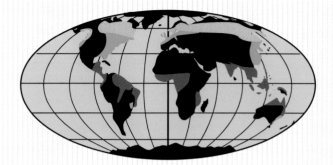

PRODUCTS

Some forests are grown especially to make products we can use.

timber for houses and furniture

chemicals

paper

food – fruit and nuts

FORESTS ARE IMPORTANT

- They provide clean air to breathe.
- The trees bind the soil and stop erosion. Erosion is when soil is washed and blown away by water and wind.
- They provide animals with a place to live.
- They provide clean water to drink.
- They provide space for recreation.

FORESTRY

Forestry is the science of planting and taking care of forests. Forestry workers are people who look after forests. They also teach other people how to look after forests.

INTERESTING FACT

Eucalyptus trees are not deciduous, but they grow in hardwood forests.

FUTURE PLANNING

Trees are grown in a plantation to provide timber to meet the needs of people.

RECREATIONAL FORESTS AND RESERVES

Some forests are recreational parks and wildlife reserves.
• People enjoy backpacking and trekking in recreational parks.
• Animals are bred at wildlife reserves.

◀ Some people live in forests. The forest provides them with everything they need.

FOSSIL

| SEE ALSO | • Coal • Dinosaur • Heritage • Mammoth • Minerals • Rocks |

A fossil is the remains of a plant or animal that lived long ago. A fossil may be a shell, a tooth, a single bone, a complete skeleton, a footprint, a print of a leaf in a rock, a single insect preserved in amber or the whole body of a dead animal.

HOW A FOSSIL IS FORMED

1. An animal dies and sinks into the seabed or swampy sand. Soft parts of the body rot away.

2. The animal skeleton is covered with layers of mud.

3. Over the years, the layers of mud turn into rock. The rocks rise above the sea.

4. The rocks are worn down. The fossil appears on the surface.

PALAEONTOLOGISTS

A palaeontologist is a scientist who digs for fossils and studies them. Fossils tell us about the past. They tell us what the land was like. Fossils tell us about the plants and animals that lived long ago.

WHERE FOSSILS ARE FOUND

Fossils are mainly found in sedimentary rock.
Some fossils are found by accident.
When you find a stone, look at it
carefully. It could be a fossil that is
millions and millions of years old.

Some fossils have been
found in the Arctic. The
dead plants and animals
were frozen thousands
of years ago.

AMMONITES ▶

Ammonites are extinct molluscs (shellfish).
They disappeared around the same time as
dinosaurs – about 65 million years ago.

FOOTPRINT FOSSILS

Long ago, dinosaurs
left footprints in mud.
Hot, melted stone from
volcanoes filled the
dinosaurs' footprints.
The stone cooled and
hardened. Many years
later, fossil hunters
digging through stone
found the footprint fossils.

INSECTS IN ▲ AMBER FOSSILS

Long ago, some insects
became caught in the
sticky gum of a tree.
The gum hardened
and became amber.
The insects were
perfectly preserved.

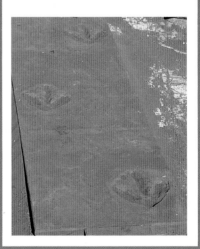

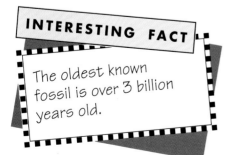

INTERESTING FACT

The oldest known
fossil is over 3 billion
years old.

FOX

SEE ALSO • Animal • Dog • Mammal

A fox is a mammal. It is a member of the dog family. Foxes hunt alone, mostly at night. In the daytime, foxes stay in their dens underground.

PARTS OF A FOX

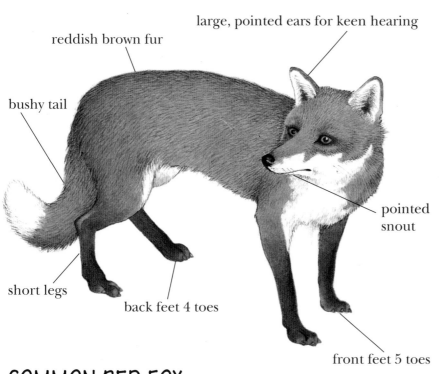

reddish brown fur

large, pointed ears for keen hearing

bushy tail

pointed snout

short legs

back feet 4 toes

front feet 5 toes

COMMON RED FOX

Average weight: 2 to 5.5 kilograms
Average length: 58 to 68 centimetres from snout to rump;
tail – 35 to 40 centimetres long

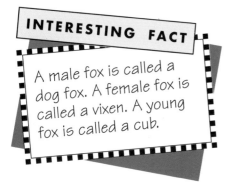

INTERESTING FACT

A male fox is called a dog fox. A female fox is called a vixen. A young fox is called a cub.

INTRODUCED FOXES

Foxes are not native animals in South America, New Zealand and Australia. They were taken there by people. Foxes hunt native animals in these countries.

KINDS OF FOXES

There are many kinds of foxes.

grey fox

red fox

bat-eared fox

Arctic fox

fennec fox

WHERE FOXES LIVE

- ● Europe
- ■ North America
- ◆ Asia – north of the Himalayas
- ★ Africa

INTERESTING FACT

Foxes that live in hot areas have larger ears. Desert foxes lose heat through their ears.

FOOD

Foxes eat other animals. They are carnivores. Foxes raid farms and eat farm animals. In cities, foxes raid rubbish bins and eat food scraps.

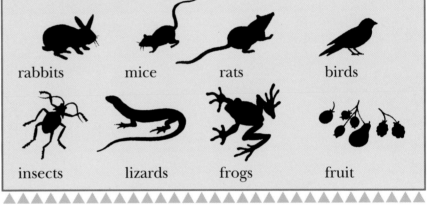

rabbits   mice   rats   birds

insects   lizards   frogs   fruit

HOW FOXES LIVE

- Foxes usually live in family groups. Sometimes, they live alone or in pairs.
- A vixen gives birth to four to ten cubs at a time. They drink milk from their mother for about eight weeks.
- When a cub is ten days old, it weighs three times as much as it did at birth.
- A newborn cub's eyes open about 14 days after birth.
- After eight weeks, cubs start to catch small animals.

FRACTION

SEE ALSO | • Measurement • Number

A fraction is a part of something.
In arithmetic, a fraction is a number.

If you cut an apple
in two, each part
of the apple is ¹/₂.

1 apple

¹/₂ an apple   ¹/₂ an apple

If you break a chocolate bar into three pieces,
each piece will be ¹/₃.

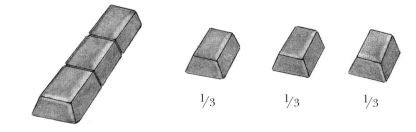

¹/₃   ¹/₃   ¹/₃

If you pour a bottle of drink equally into four
glasses, each glass will contain ¹/₄ of the bottle.

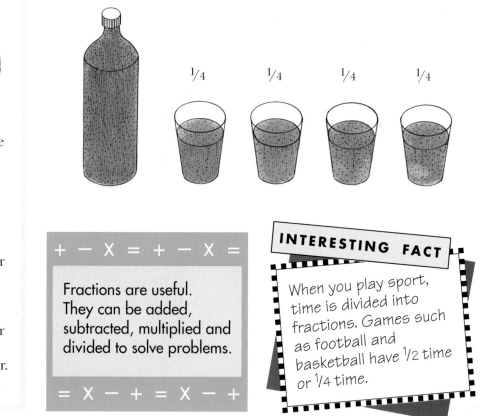

¹/₄   ¹/₄   ¹/₄   ¹/₄

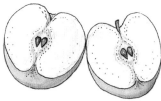

1 ← This number is called the numerator.

2 ← This number is called the denominator.

+ − X = + − X =

Fractions are useful.
They can be added,
subtracted, multiplied and
divided to solve problems.

= X − + = X − +

INTERESTING FACT

When you play sport,
time is divided into
fractions. Games such
as football and
basketball have ¹/₂ time
or ¹/₄ time.

FRICTION

SEE ALSO • Motor Car • Oil • Train

Friction happens when objects move over one another.

FRICTION CAN CREATE HEAT

When you rub two things together, you create friction. Rub your hands together quickly. They will get hot. The heat has been made by friction.

TRAINS ▼

Train wheels and train tracks are smooth. This cuts down on friction so trains can move faster.

OIL

Oil reduces friction. It makes it easier for objects to move over each other. Friction creates heat which can wear down the moving parts of engines. Oil is used to cut down friction and heat.

FRICTION IS IMPORTANT

• You can walk because there is friction between your shoes and the ground. Walking on ice is hard. The smooth surface of ice creates less friction than a footpath.
• Nails stay in wood because of friction.
• Car wheels move the car because of the friction between the wheels and the surface of the road. Without friction, wheels would just spin around and the car would not move.

FROG

SEE ALSO
• Animal • Amphibians
• Life Cycle

A frog is an amphibian. A frog starts its life in fresh water breathing through gills. Adult frogs have lungs and can breathe air.

PARTS OF A FROG

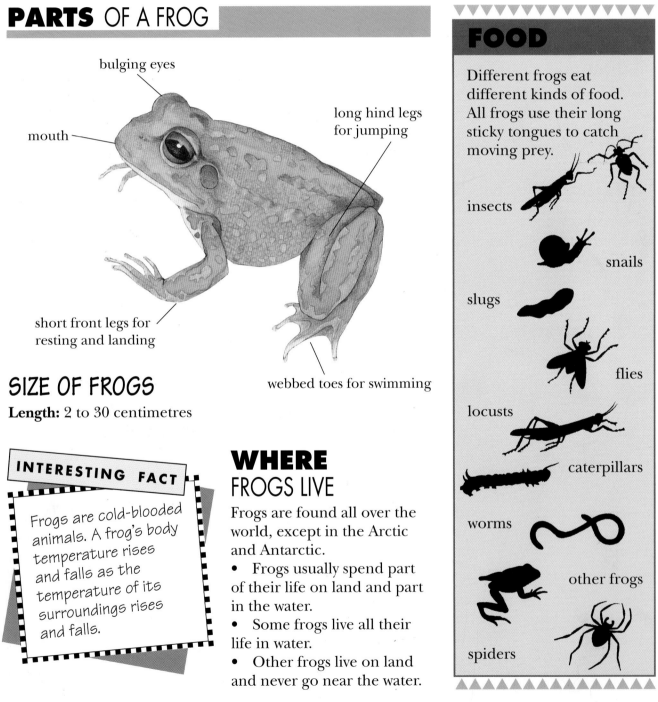

bulging eyes

mouth

long hind legs for jumping

short front legs for resting and landing

webbed toes for swimming

SIZE OF FROGS

Length: 2 to 30 centimetres

INTERESTING FACT

Frogs are cold-blooded animals. A frog's body temperature rises and falls as the temperature of its surroundings rises and falls.

WHERE FROGS LIVE

Frogs are found all over the world, except in the Arctic and Antarctic.
• Frogs usually spend part of their life on land and part in the water.
• Some frogs live all their life in water.
• Other frogs live on land and never go near the water.

FOOD

Different frogs eat different kinds of food. All frogs use their long sticky tongues to catch moving prey.

insects

snails

slugs

flies

locusts

caterpillars

worms

other frogs

spiders

HOW FROGS LIVE

- Frogs lay several hundred eggs in jelly in water.
- Tadpoles hatch from the eggs after about ten days. Tadpoles swim like fish and breathe through gills.
- The tadpoles develop legs and lungs, and lose their tail.

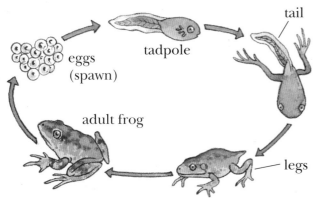

eggs (spawn)

tadpole

tail

adult frog

legs

KINDS OF FROGS

There are more than 2500 kinds of frogs.
- The goliath frog lives in central Africa. It weighs three kilograms.
- Tree frogs are only two centimetres long. They live in trees. Suckers on the end of their feet help them climb trees.

▼

FROGS AND TOADS

- Frogs have smooth skin.
- Toads have dark, rough skin which is often covered in warts.
- A frog hops, while a toad crawls or runs.
- A toad has a broader, flatter body than a frog.

toad

frog

WHY FROGS ARE IMPORTANT

Frogs help people by eating insects. Some frogs are becoming endangered. They are protected by law.

INTERESTING FACT

A common frog can jump as far as 60 centimetres. This is six to seven times its own body length.

FRUIT

SEE ALSO • Farming • Flower • Food • Nut • Plant

Fruit comes from flowers. The fruit contains the seeds. The fruit protects the seeds until they are ready to grow into new plants.

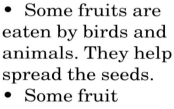

• Some fruits are eaten by birds and animals. They help spread the seeds.
• Some fruit seeds have wings that help the wind carry the seed away.

WHERE FRUIT GROWS

Fruit grows all over the world, except in the Arctic and Antarctic.

DIFFERENT KINDS OF FRUIT

• Some fruits cannot be eaten.

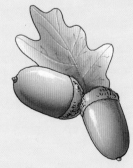

oak acorn

• A nut is a hard-cased fruit. The part of the nut we eat is the seed.

walnut

• Some fruits are pods and some have wings or hairs.

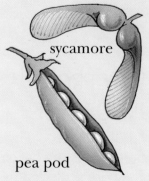

sycamore

pea pod

• Berries are small, juicy fruits with pips inside. Grapes are one type of berry.

HOW A PEACH RIPENS

The fruit grows from the flower of a plant.
As the fruit grows, the sepals and petals fall off.

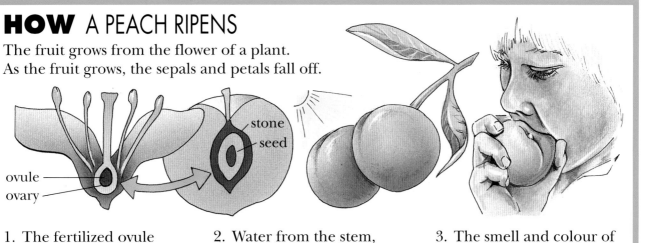

ovule
ovary

stone
seed

1. The fertilized ovule grows into the seed. The surrounding ovary becomes the stone. The stone protects the seed.

2. Water from the stem, and energy from the Sun make the juicy covering of the fruit.

3. The smell and colour of the peach attract animals and people. They eat the juicy outside and throw away the stone.

KINDS OF FRUIT WE EAT

There are many different kinds of fruit.
Different fruits grow in different climates.

Tropical fruit

banana   pineapple

mango   passionfruit

Sub-tropical fruit

orange   lemon   grapefruit

fig   date   olive

Temperate fruit

grape   apple   pear

plum   peach   berry

ORCHARDS ▲

The fruit we buy in shops is grown in orchards.
When it is ripe, farmers send the fruit to markets for people to buy.

61

FUEL

SEE ALSO
• Coal • Electricity • Gas
• Oil • Water • Wind

Fuel gives us energy. It provides power and heat when it is burnt. People use three main kinds of fuel – coal, oil and natural gas. These fuels come from under the ground.

FUEL IS ENERGY ▲

Fuel provides energy to:
- heat houses and buildings
- cook food
- make electricity
- power ships, planes, cars and machines.

INTERESTING FACT

Once, coal was the most important fuel. Now, oil is the most important fuel. Modern transport uses oil for fuel.

THE GREENHOUSE EFFECT

Burning fossil fuels harms the environment.

- Fossil fuels give off carbon dioxide.
- Carbon dioxide builds up in the atmosphere. It stops heat from the Earth escaping into space.
- If the Earth becomes warmer, the polar ice caps will melt. Sea levels will rise and flood low-lying land.

some heat escapes into space

Sun

gases

some heat is absorbed

some heat is trapped by the gases

FOSSIL FUELS

Coal, oil and natural gas come from under the ground. They are fossil fuels. They were formed from the remains of prehistoric plants and animals. Some fossil fuels are starting to run out.

NEW ENERGY ▲ FOR POWER

Wind power, solar power and hydro-electricity are cheap forms of energy and do not create pollution.

FUNGI

SEE ALSO • Drug • Forest

Mushrooms, toadstools and mould are fungi. Fungi look like plants, but they do not have roots, leaves or flowers.

PARTS OF A MUSHROOM

The mushroom we see is the fruit of the fungus. The mushroom contains the spores.

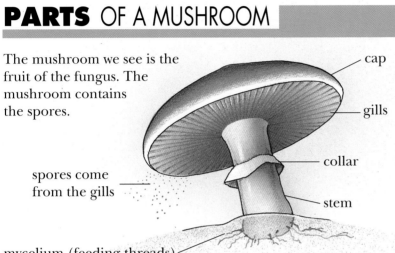

cap

gills

spores come from the gills

collar

stem

mycelium (feeding threads)

Fungi cannot make their own food like plants can. They feed on dead or living plants or animals.

POISONOUS ▼ FUNGI

Some fungi are poisonous to eat. Fly agaric fungus is a poisonous mushroom.

HOW A FUNGUS GROWS

Fungi produce dust-like spores. The spores are scattered by the wind. Each spore grows into a new fungus.

KINDS OF FUNGI

- Yeast is a fungus which is used to make drinks and bread.
- Many mushrooms and truffles can be eaten.
- Mould is a fungus. You can see mould growing on old bread.

FUNGI ARE IMPORTANT

Fungi are used in medicines such as antibiotics. The medicines are used to treat illness and disease.